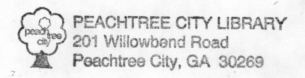

A ROOKIE BIOGRAPHY

MARTIN LUTHER KING, JR.

A Man Who Changed Things

By Carol Greene

CHILDRENS PRESS®

CHICAGO

This book is for James Mann.

**Martin
Luther King, Jr.
(1929-1968)**

LIBRARY OF CONGRESS
Library of Congress Cataloging-in-Publication Data

Greene, Carol.
    Martin Luther King, Jr. : a man who changed things / by Carol Greene
    p. cm. — (A Rookie biography)
    Summary: A simple biography of the Baptist minister and civil rights
leader who helped American blacks win many battles for equal rights
and who was awarded the Nobel Peace Prize in 1964.
    ISBN 0-516-04205-X
    1. King, Martin Luther, Jr., 1929-1968—Juvenile literature. 2. Afro-
Americans—Biography—Juvenile literature. 3. Baptists—United
States—Clergy—Biography—Juvenile literature. 4. Civil rights
workers—United States—Biography—Juvenile literature. 5. Afro-
Americans—Civil rights—Juvenile literature. [1. King, Martin Luther,
Jr., 1929-1968. 2. Civil rights workers. 3. Clergy. 4. Afro-Americans—
Biography.] I. Title. II. Series: Greene, Carol. Rookie biography.
E185.97.K5G74   1989
323.4′092′4—dc19
[B]
[92]   88-37714
                                           CIP
                                          AC

Martin Luther King, Jr.,
was a real person.
He lived from 1929 to 1968.
He believed that all people
should be free and equal.
And he believed in peace.
This is his story.

TABLE OF CONTENTS

M.L. was born in this house.

Chapter 1

A Hard Question

M.L. ran to his friends' house.
His real name was
Martin Luther King, Jr.
But everyone called him M.L.
He was six years old.

His friends' mother
came to the door.
"You can't play together
anymore," she said.
"We're white and you're colored."

M.L. began to cry.
He didn't understand.
So he ran home.

"Why, Mother Dear?" he asked.
"Why can't we play?"

Mother Dear wanted to cry, too.
She told M.L. how white people
brought black people to America.
They made black people slaves.

Then in 1863,
the United States government
said black people were free.
But some white people
still thought they were better
than black people.

Opposite page: The Emancipation Proclamation was signed by Abraham Lincoln.
The Proclamation said that all the slaves that lived in the Confederate states would
be set free on January 1, 1863 unless the South stopped fighting before that date.

M.L.'s family: Standing from left to right, are his mother, Alberta Williams King; his father, Martin Luther King, Sr.; his grandmother, Jennie Williams. Sitting from left to right, his brother, Alfred Daniel; his sister, Christine; and Martin.

"You are just as good
as anyone else,"
Mother Dear told M.L.
"And don't you forget it!"

So M.L. played
with his big sister, Chris,
and his little brother, A.D.

Once M.L. and A.D.
were playing baseball
with other black children.
A.D. was batting
and M.L. was catching.

All at once, the bat
flew out of A.D.'s hands.
It hit M.L. on the head
and knocked him down.
M.L. popped right back up.

"You're out!" he said.
He was *tough*.

Daddy King (above) was pastor of the Ebenezer Baptist Church (below).

M.L.'s father, Daddy King, was pastor of Ebenezer Baptist Church in Atlanta, Georgia. The King family spent a lot of time at church.

But most of all, M.L. liked
to be with his grandmother.
Mama Williams talked to him
about God and the Bible.
She tried to answer his questions.

M.L. had lots of questions.
But the hardest one
was still "Why?"
Why couldn't black people
and white people be equal?
Why couldn't things be different?

When M.L. was a young boy, black people
could not sit next to white people on the bus.

Chapter 2

Some Answers

M.L. started high school
when he was only 13.
Everyone said,
"M.L. will be a minister."
M.L. wanted to be a doctor.

In high school, M.L. won
a speech contest.
He and his teacher
rode home on a bus.
The bus filled.
The driver came to them.

"Get up," he said.
"Give your seats to white
people."

13

"No," said M.L.

He wasn't afraid.
But his teacher
looked ready to cry.
M.L. got up for her sake.

When he was 15, M.L. went
to Morehouse College in Atlanta.
Now people called him Martin.

"Martin will be a minister,"
they said.
He wanted to be a lawyer.

Martin had good teachers.
They let him ask questions.
He learned that ministers
can do many things.
When he was 17, Martin said,
"I will be a minister."

So after college, he went
to school in Pennsylvania.
He studied to be a minister.
He made all A's.
But he still had questions.

Crozer Theological Seminary in
Chester, Pennsylvania

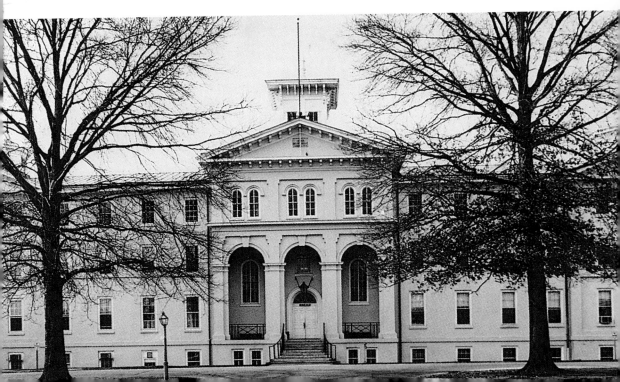

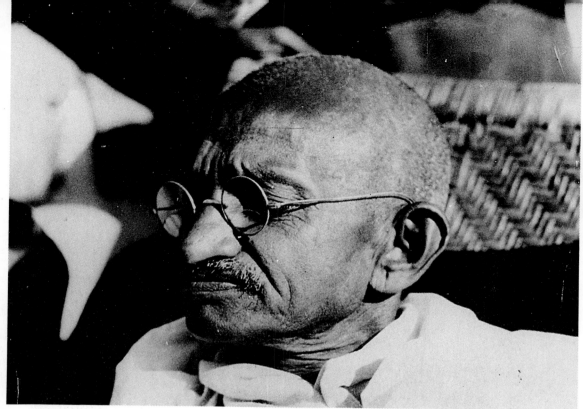

Mahatma Gandhi led the people of India to independence from English rule. He believed that nonviolent protests could bring about great changes.

"Love your enemies,"
said the Bible.
"How can I do that?"
asked Martin.

Then he heard
about a man in India.
His name was Gandhi.
Gandhi believed in love.
He would not hurt anyone.
But he changed things.

Now Martin had an answer.
He would love his enemies.
But he would hate
the bad things they did.
And he would change things, too.

Coretta Scott married
Martin in 1953.

Chapter 3

Changing Things

++

Next, Martin studied in Boston.
There he met a girl.
Her name was Coretta Scott.
She was pretty *and* smart.
On their first date, Martin
asked her to marry him.

She didn't say yes right away.
But in 1953, they got married.
In 1954, they moved
to Montgomery, Alabama.

Martin became
minister at
Dexter Avenue
Baptist Church.
Black people had
a hard time
in Alabama.
He wanted
to help them.

In 1955, a city bus driver
told Mrs. Rosa Parks
to give her seat
to a white man.
She said, "No."
She was arrested.

Opposite page:
On December 1, 1955
Rosa Park was arrested,
fingerprinted,
and put in jail
because she refused
to give up her seat
on a segregated bus.

"We won't ride buses until the laws change," said Montgomery's black people. For almost a year, they did not ride buses. They walked or rode in car pools.

Young girl (above) hitches a ride. The Montgomery bus boycott was organized by Dr. Martin Luther King, Jr. and others. When it was over, the buses in Montgomery were no longer segregated.

Although Dr. King believed
in nonviolence, his enemies
did not. Crosses were burned
on his lawn and his house
was bombed. Neither of these acts
caused Martin Luther King, Jr.
to give up.

Martin preached
sermons and made
speeches to help.
His house was
bombed. But
no one got hurt.

At last, the United States
Supreme Court said
the laws were wrong.
Now black people could
ride like white people.

After President Johnson signed
the Civil Rights Act of 1964,
he shook Dr. King's hand.

Martin Luther King was president of the Southern Christian Leadership Conference.

In 1957, black ministers
in the South formed a group,
the Southern Christian
Leadership Conference
(SCLC, for short).
They elected Martin president.

Martin preached at his father's church in Atlanta.

In 1959, he moved
back to Atlanta.
He worked at Daddy King's church
and with the SCLC.

At that time, black people
and white people couldn't eat
at the same lunch counter.
Martin and others
sat together anyway.

Martin Luther King, Jr.
was arrested and put
in jail many times.

They were peaceful.
But sometimes police
arrested them.
That happened to Martin
in 1960.

But he still begged people
to be peaceful.
"Love your enemies," he said.

By 1961, the Kings
had three children:
Yoki, Marty, and Dexter.
One day, Yoki wanted to go
to a park called Funtown.

She couldn't, said Martin.
No black children could.
Yoki cried.
So did Martin.

Then he remembered
what Mother Dear had told
him. He hugged his little
girl. "You are as good as
anyone," he said.

From left to right: Yolanda (Yoki),
Martin Luther King III (Marty),
Dexter, and Bernice Albertine

Fire hoses, police dogs,
and billy clubs were
used to break up
peaceful demonstrations.

Chapter 4

"I Have a Dream!"

Laws in Birmingham, Alabama,
said black people had to use
different lunch counters,
restrooms, and water fountains.
In 1963, the SCLC decided
to hold peaceful marches
to change these laws.

Martin helped lead them.
He was arrested.
He saw children arrested, too.
Firemen knocked them down
with water from fire hoses.
Police set dogs on them.

The marchers
didn't stop.
They *prayed* for
their enemies.
News programs
showed everyone
what was happening.
Then one day,
something different
happened.

"Turn them hoses on!"
yelled the head policeman,
Bull Conners.
But the firemen and
the police did nothing.

The march went on
and soon the laws changed.

Later that year,
black people and white people
marched in Washington, D.C.
Martin spoke to them.

"I have a dream," he said.
He dreamed that one day
all Americans would be equal.

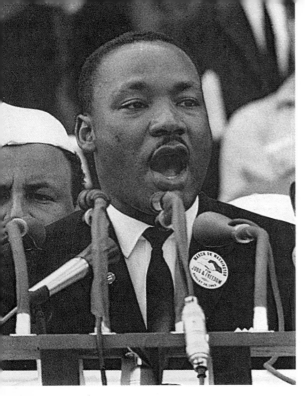

"I have a dream!" he cried.
The people cried, "Amen!"
"Let freedom ring!"
he shouted.
The people shouted too.

Dr. King spoke from the
steps of the Lincoln Memorial.

One day, said Martin,
all of God's children
would join hands and sing:
"Free at last! Free at last!
Thank God Almighty,
we are free at last!"

The crowd was quiet.
Then they cheered and cheered.

At the end of that year,
something else happened.
It happened quietly.
But it was very important
to Martin.

He took Yoki to Funtown.
Black children could
go there now.

Martin Luther King, Jr. accepts the Nobel Peace Prize (above).
Later he and Coretta talked to reporters.

Chapter 5

Free at Last

Martin made
more speeches.
He led more
marches.
He helped people
become voters.
Sometimes
he went to jail.

In 1964, Martin won
the Nobel Peace Prize.
He shouted for joy.
His whole family went
to Norway with him
to get the prize.

**Dr. Martin Luther King, Jr. led blacks and
whites on the long march from Selma to Montgomery.**

Then he got back
to work. He set up
a march from Selma
to Montgomery,
Alabama.
Three marchers
were killed.
Still Martin
begged people
to be peaceful.

Dr. King walks with
the Reverend Ralph Abernathy,
a fellow civil rights leader.

He wanted to help
poor black people
in northern cities.
But he wanted to do it peacefully.
Some other black leaders
did not agree with him.

By 1968, Martin felt
sad and tired.
His friends told him
he had changed many things.
He wasn't so sure.

He led a march
in Memphis, Tennessee.
Some marchers got rough.
Martin left the march.
"I will never be in front
of a violent march," he said.

On April 4, Martin stood
outside his motel room.
A shot rang out
and he fell.
He died in a Memphis hospital.
He was 39 years old.

Martin Luther King, Jr. shown on the balcony of his
Memphis hotel the day before he was shot. From left to right:
Hosea Williams, Jesse Jackson, Dr. King, Reverend Ralph Abernathy

People everywhere cried.
Some became violent.
An escaped prisoner,
James Earl Ray, was
found guilty of the murder.

Dr. King's coffin was carried on a farm wagon pulled by two Georgia mules.
More than 50,000 people attended his funeral in Atlanta, Georgia.

Martin Luther King, Jr.,
was buried in Atlanta.
He *had* changed
many things,
even people's
hearts.

The stone on his grave says:
"Free at last. Free at last.
Thank God Almighty
I'm free at last."

Important Dates

1929   January 15—Born in Atlanta, Georgia to
        Martin Luther and Alberta King

1944   Entered Morehouse College, Atlanta

1953   Married Coretta Scott

1954   Became pastor of Dexter Avenue Baptist
        Church, Montgomery, Alabama

1955   Led bus boycott in Montgomery

1957   Became president of the SCLC

1959   Moved to Atlanta

1963   Gave "I have a dream . . ." speech,
        Washington, D.C.

1964   Won Nobel Peace Prize

1965   Led march from Selma to Montgomery

1968   April 4—Killed by James Earl Ray in
        Memphis, Tennessee

INDEX

Page numbers in boldface type indicate illustrations.

PHOTO CREDITS

ABOUT THE AUTHOR

Carol Greene has degrees in English Literature and Musicology. She has worked in international exchange programs, as an editor, and as a teacher. She now lives in St. Louis, Missouri, and writes full time. She has published more than seventy books. Other Childrens Press biographies by Ms. Greene include *Louisa May Alcott, Marie Curie, Thomas Alva Edison, Hans Christian Andersen, Marco Polo,* and *Wolfgang Amadeus Mozart* in the People of Distinction series, *Sandra Day O'Connor, Mother Teresa, Indira Nehru Gandhi, Diana, Princess of Wales, Desmond Tutu,* and *Elie Wiesel* in the Picture-Story Biography series, and *Benjamin Franklin, Pocahontas,* and *Christopher Columbus* in the Rookie Biographies.